The Boy Jesus
Goes A-Walking

and Other Stories

The Boy Jesus Goes A-Walking
and Other Stories

Written by Mary Richardson
Illustrated by Hilda Joanna

PAULIST PRESS
New York / Mahwah, N.J.

First published in Great
Britain in 1976 by
Mayhew McCrimmon Ltd
Great Wakering Essex. © Copyright 1976
and 1985 by Mayhew McCrimmon Ltd.

First published in the United States of
America by Paulist Press copyright
© 1988

ISBN: 0-8091-6575-9

Published by
Paulist Press
997 Macarthur Boulevard
Mahwah, New Jersey 07430

Printed and bound in the U.S.A.

Contents

The Boy Jesus Goes A-Walking

Ruth and Silas
got up early.
The sky had been so red
that their father said,
"There'll be a storm today,"
But the wind
was in the south
and the sun was hot
as they went along
to Joseph's house.

"Can Jesus come and
  play with us?" they asked.
  Joseph said,
"There's not much work today.
  Run along, son,
  and have a good walk
  with your friends."

They walked away
from the village.
There was a hen
in the road,
with all her chickens
pecking up grain.
When she saw
the three children
she clucked a warning
and the chickens
all came running
and hid under her wings.

They passed by the sheepfolds.
Shepherds were still sitting
at the entrances.
"They're keeping the wolves
away," said Silas.
One shepherd
had been out all night,
looking for a lamb
that had got lost.
They saw him coming home,
tattered and tired but happy
carrying the silly little lamb.
"That's a good shepherd,"
said Ruth.

The vines in the vineyards
were growing well.
"There are some by the
side of the path," said Ruth.
"Perhaps they'll have
grapes on them."
"Silly," said Silas,
"those are thorn bushes.
You don't get grapes on them."
"You only get good grapes
if the vines are pruned,"
said Jesus.

They stopped to look at
the golden cornfields.
"My dad will have to find
lots of men to help him
to reap," said Silas.
"He planted good seed
but some enemy must
have sown weeds in it."
"Now it's harvest time,
they can gather the corn
and burn the weeds,"
said Jesus.

"Look at those straggly plants
  in the thornbushes," said Ruth.
"And the ones that have
  withered on the rock,"
  said Silas.
"I guess the birds
  had a good feed."
"But the seeds have
  grown very well
  in the fields," said Jesus.

"Seeds are very strange,"
  said Ruth.
"You put them
  into the ground and go away
  and then one day
  they push up,
  all alive and growing."
"And don't they grow!"
  said Silas.
"The tiny mustard seed
  makes that great bush over there,
  with all the birds on it."

"Quiet!" said Silas.
A fox was padding softly by,
his sharp ears pricked,
his russet body cunningly
moving on his way
to a hen house.
"I'll show you where he lives,"
said Jesus.
He led them up the hillside
and showed them a hole
in the ground.
"He'll be safe in his
home inside there," he said.

Bright anemones were growing
in every cranny of the rocks.
Ruth began picking them.
Silas watched the larks
singing high in the sky
and the little sparrows
scuffling about among the
bushes for their food.
"Lucky things," he said.
"They don't have to work
for their living."
"God looks after them,"
Jesus said.

A dark cloud hid the sun.
"Here comes the storm
my dad said we'd get,"
said Silas.
"We're going to get wet,"
said Ruth.
"Yes, the rain will fall
on us, whether we're
good or naughty," said Jesus.
"But we'd better make haste."
So thay ran home
as fast as they could
to Jesus's house.

His mother had just mixed
a tiny bit of yeast
into a bowl of flour.
They watched the lumps of
dough get bigger
and bigger and bigger.

Then Jesus's mother
made it into loaves
and baked them in her oven.
They came out lovely
and hot and crispy
and she gave them to the
children to share.
They did enjoy them.

And afterwards,
when Jesus was grown-up,
he remembered
all the things he had seen,
and he told us about them,
and they were all written down
by his friends
Matthew, Mark, Luke and John,
and one day
you will read them
in their books.

Jesus and the
Two Blind Men

There were two men
sitting at the side of a road.
It ran down between
hills and trees,
to a town with big houses.
But the two men
didn't see the road,
or the hills,
or the trees,
or the houses.

Birds flew above them
in the blue sky,
but they didn't see them.
Sheep cropped the grass
on the hillside behind them.
Little ants ran in and out
of the stones beside them,
but they didn't see them.

Sometimes soldiers
with flashing helmets
and swords and shields,
marched along the road,
but they didn't see them.

Sometimes merchants on
camels rode by,
with baggage piled high,
but they didn't see them.

And the two men
couldn't see to do any work,
or earn any money,
for their food
or their clothes,
for they were blind.

So each day
they shuffled along
to the edge of the road,
and sat there.
And people going along the
road saw them
and sometimes they were
sorry for them,
and gave them a penny.

And sometimes
they weren't sorry for them,
and didn't give them a penny.

One day
the two blind men
heard a lot of noise,
and the sound of many feet
coming along the road
from the town.
"It's Jesus,
the prophet from Nazareth,"
the people in the crowd
told them.
"He's cured lots of people
who were ill."

So the two blind men
began shouting:
"Lord be sorry for us!
Son of David, be sorry for us!
Jesus of Nazareth,
be sorry for us!"

"Oh do be quiet,"
  the people in the crowd said.
"Don't shout out like that.
  Keep quiet."

The two blind men said,
"Keep quiet yourselves,"
and they began shouting
even more loudly,
"Lord, be sorry for us!
"Son of David, be sorry for us!"
Jesus stopped.
"Come over here to me,"
he said.

The two blind men
groped their way
through the crowd,
to the sound of his voice.
"What do you want me
to do for you?" he asked.
The two blind men said,
"Lord, let us be able
to see again."

Jesus put out his hands
and touched their eyes.
At once the blackness
of their blindness disappeared,
and they could see!
And the first thing they saw
was the kind, smiling face
of Jesus.

"Thank you, Son of David,"
they said,
and when he walked on again,
they followed him,
laughing for joy.
For now they could see
the merchants
and the soldiers, and the ants,
and the sheep,
and the birds in the blue sky,
and the houses, and the trees,
and the hills, and the road —
but best of all,
they could see Jesus.

The Little Man in the Tree

What a lot of noise
there was in the
streets of Jericho!

"What's it all about?"
asked Zacchaeus.
He was a short little man
and he had
a great deal of money.

"It's Jesus,
   the prophet from Nazareth,"
   they told him.
"We've heard a lot about him.
   Everyone's hurrying along
   to see him."

"Oh dear!" thought Zacchaeus,
"I'm much too short
   to see him in all this crowd.
   But I know what I will do."

He ran right ahead,
in front of the crowd
and when he came
to a sycamore tree
at the side of the road,
he climbed up it
and sat astride a branch.
"Now I shall see better
than anyone," he said.

Soon all the people
came pushing
and squeezing
and shoving each other,
and there was Jesus
right in the middle of them all.

When Jesus got as far as
the sycamore tree, he stopped.
He looked straight
at the rich little man and said,
"Come down, Zacchaeus,
and be quick.
I've got to stay
at your house today."

Zacchaeus slid down the tree
as fast as he could.
"Jesus," he said,
"I'm ever so pleased.
Come along with me
and I'll call some
of my friends together
and we'll have
a real fine dinner."

Some of the people
in the crowd said,
"Go with Zacchaeus?
He's a bad man.
Goodness knows how
he got all his money.
And his friends are
all a lot of scallywags.
Don't go with him."

But Zacchaeus said,
"Maybe I've not always
  been good,
  but now I've seen you, Jesus,
  I'm going to be better."

"Look sir, I'm going
to give half
of everything I have
to poor people,
and, sir, if I've
cheated anyone,
I'll give him back
four times as much."

"You are the sort of person
  I go looking for," said Jesus.
"I'm coming straight home
  to your house with you."

So Jesus and Zacchaeus
and all his scallywag friends
sat down together
and had a fine meal
and enjoyed being
with each other
all that day.

When the children came
crowding round the open door,
to see all the fun
that was going on,
Zacchaeus gave them all
a share of the goodies,
so everyone
was very happy.